What if... We were pilots?

The Project Book for Role Play in Early Years Settings

Published 2009 by A&C Black Publishers Limited
36 Soho Square, London W1D 3QY
www.acblack.com

ISBN 978-1-4081-1251-9

A CIP record for this publication is available from the British Library.

Acknowledgements
Thank you for the following parties for their help in producing the materials in this book:
Headcorn Aerodrome in Kent
Thurston Helicopters Ltd

Printed in the UK by Latimer Trend & Company Ltd

This book is produced using paper that is made from wood grown in
managed, sustainable forests. It is natural, renewable and recyclable.
The logging and manufacturing processes conform to the environmental
regulations of the country of origin.

To see our full range of titles

visit **www.acblack.com/featherstone**

Contents

Introduction

What if? project books offer practitioners a wide and flexible range of resources for role play, involving children in playing out well known everyday situations and exploring those which may be less familiar. They help you make the most of an activity which all children love – pretend play and playing in a role. *What if?* project books are ideal for extending language, creativity and active learning. All materials are suitable for work in the Early Years Foundation Stage (EYFS) and Key Stage 1, with the relevant EYFS Key Early Learning Goals clearly outlined.

Each project book includes:

- A wealth of print, pictorial and photographic resources which can be used flexibly to provide children with starting points and further stimuli for expanding their play.
- A real-life photo story told in high quality photographs and short text, providing you with a resource to enrich role play and to extend children's experiences through a strong non-fiction 'story line'.
- An accompanying CD-ROM of the photo story in a Powerpoint presentation, an extended Powerpoint presentation featuring a sequence of photographs with descriptive text, artwork and activity sheets. All can be projected on to an interactive whiteboard or viewed on a computer, or printed out to enhance your play.
- Practitioners' advice on how to prepare for and conduct safe and enjoyable visits.
- Resource and equipment suggestions to support learning – with an emphasis on affordability.
- Useful websites, DVDs and books, songs and rhymes, including the *What if?* series theme tune and song!

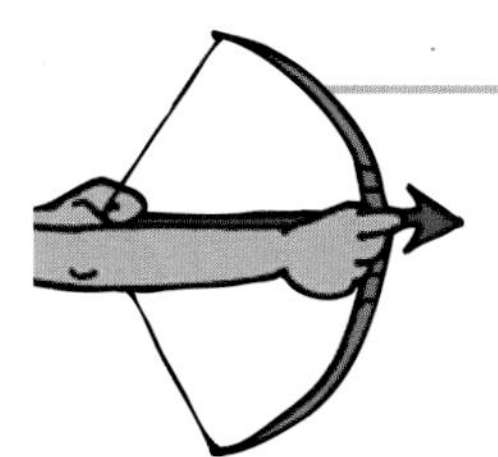

Key Early Learning Goals

The EYFS Early Learning Goals linked to *What if... We were pilots?* and to the activities suggested are:

PERSONAL, SOCIAL AND EMOTIONAL DEVELOPMENT

- Continue to be interested, excited and motivated to learn;
- Be confident to try new activities, initiate ideas and speak in a familiar group;
- Work as part of a group or class, taking turns and sharing fairly, understanding that there needs to be agreed values and codes of behaviour for groups of people (including adults and children) to work together harmoniously;
- Dress and undress independently;
- Select and use activities and resources independently.

COMMUNICATION, LANGUAGE AND LITERACY

- Interact with others, negotiating plans and activities, taking turns in conversations;
- Enjoy listening to and using spoken and written language, and readily turn to it in their play and learning;
- Listen with enjoyment and respond to stories, songs, other music, rhymes and poems and make up their own stories, rhymes and poems;
- Extend their vocabulary; exploring the meanings and sounds of new words;
- Use language to imagine and recreate roles and experiences;
- Use talk to organise, sequence and clarify thinking, ideas, feelings and events;
- Retell narratives in the correct sequence drawing on the language patterns of stories;
- Attempt writing for various purposes, using features of different forms such as lists, stories, instructions.

PROBLEM SOLVING, REASONING AND NUMERACY

- Say and use number names in order in familiar contexts;
- Recognise numerals 1-9;
- Use everyday words to describe position.

PHYSICAL DEVELOPMENT

- Move with confidence, imagination and in safety;
- Move with control and coordination;
- Travel around, under, over and through balancing and climbing equipment;
- Show awareness of space, both of themselves and of others;
- Use a range of small and large equipment;
- Handle tools, objects, construction and malleable materials safely and with increasing control.

KNOWLEDGE AND UNDERSTANDING OF THE WORLD

- Investigate objects and materials by using all of their senses as appropriate;
- Find out about, and identify some features of living things, objects and events they observe;
- Ask questions about why things happen and how things work;
- Build and construct with a wide range of objects, selecting appropriate resources and adapting their work where necessary;
- Select tools and techniques they need to shape, assemble and join the materials they are using;
- Find out about and identify the uses of technology in their everyday lives and use computers and programmed toys to support their learning;
- Observe, find out about and identify features in the place they live and the natural world.

CREATIVE DEVELOPMENT

- Recognise and explore how sounds can be changed, sing simple songs from memory, recognise repeated sounds and sound patterns and match movements to music;
- Use their imagination in art and design, music, dance, imaginative and role play and stories;
- Respond in a variety of ways to what they see, hear, smell, touch and feel;
- Express and communicate their ideas, thoughts and feelings by using a widening range of materials, suitable tools, imaginative and role play, movement, designing and making, and a variety of songs and instruments.

What if... We were pilots?

The Photo Story

How to Use the Photo Story

Read the story right through first. This will help children to understand the whole story. When you have read the story, you could go back to some of the people, activities and objects in the book. Don't try to do them all in one session, and follow the children's interests, spending more time on these.

Here are some ideas:

- Ask some 'thinking questions', such as: 'Why do you need a fire engine at an airport?'; 'How does the pilot know which way to go?'; 'How do the crew know if they have enough food for the flight?'; 'What are headphones for?'; 'Why do flight crew have uniforms?'; 'Where do the crew eat their meals?'; 'What are the dials on the instrument panel do?'
- What sort of clothes and shoes would you wear to go on a plane? Why do you need these clothes? What would you take in your hand luggage?

- Look carefully at the pictures of planes and helicopters. What is the difference between them?
- Talk about the different people in the book. Can the children remember their names and their jobs?
- Look at all the people who are NOT pilots. What are they doing? Why are they needed? What would happen if they didn't come to work? How do they learn how to do their special jobs?

- Look at all the signs, notices and badges. Read them together and talk about what each is for. You could make badges and signs for your own airport game.
- Talk about how you could make a plane or an airport in your role play area or outside. What will you need? Where could you find the materials and equipment? What could the children make themselves? Look at the plans, resources and information on the CD, as well as the photo story and Powerpoint presentation to help them think.

- Talk about all the places that planes go. Look at an atlas or globe together and discuss destinations. Use a search engine to find pictures of airports in different countries. What is the same and what is different about these places? Find some unusual airports and airfields – in the desert, in the Antarctic, on an island.

Let's be pilots!

We'll start by visiting Headcorn Aerodrome

It is a small aerodrome with a grass runway.

It also has a helipad for helicopters to land and take off.

The pilots have headsets with radios so they can talk to Air Traffic Control.

Ray is the Air Traffic Controller. He helps the pilots fly safely.

All the pilots and staff can listen to Ray on their radios for airport information.

Every aeroplane in the world has its own special registration number

Every time an aircraft lands, Ray writes the registration in his logbook.

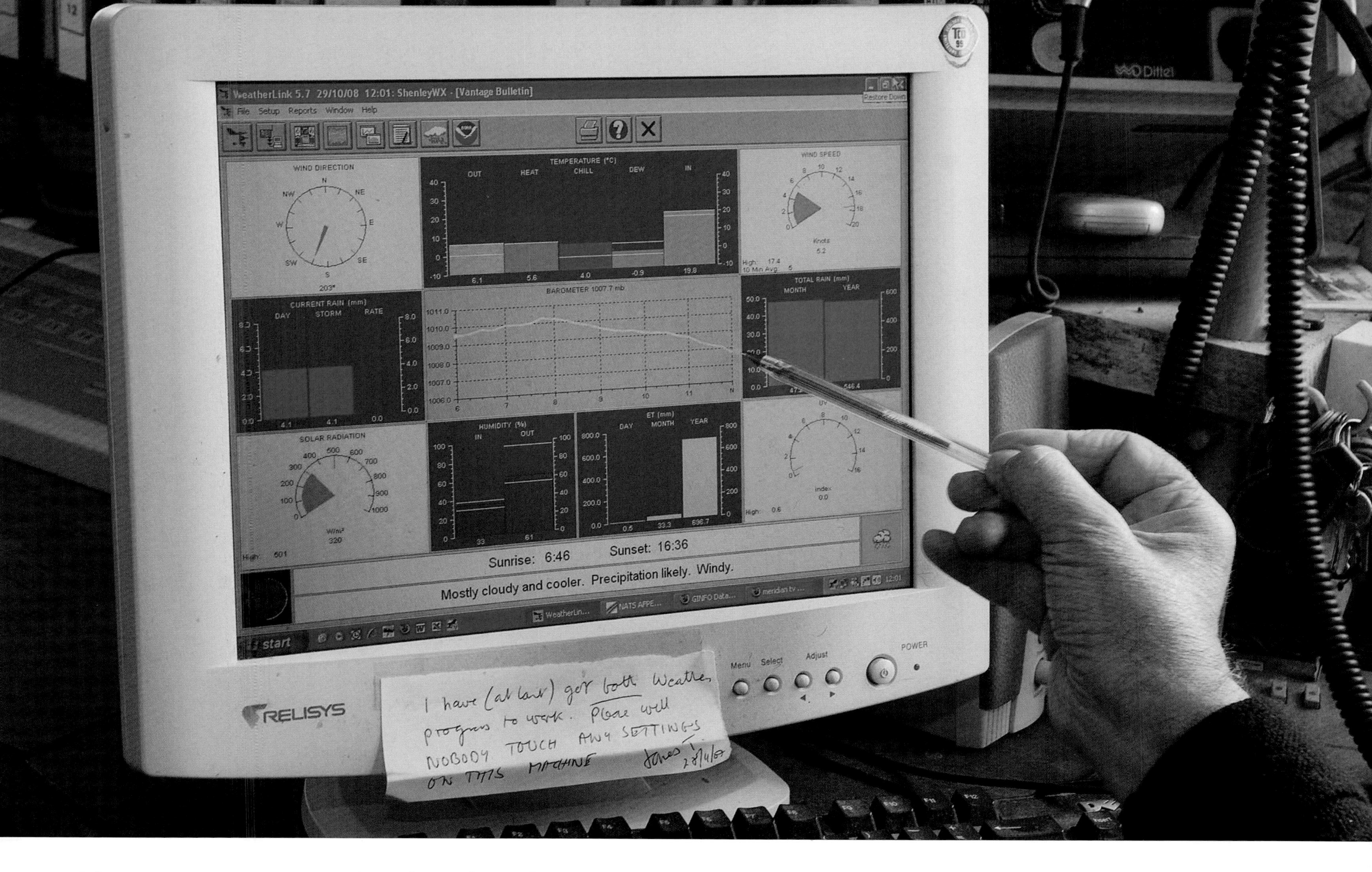

He uses a computer to check weather conditions, wind speed and direction

Pilots can also look at the windsock to see if it is too windy to take off.

Fences keep visitors, cars and animals safely away from the runway.

Only pilots, passengers and airport staff are allowed beyond the fence.

These signs help pilots and visitors find their way around the aerodrome

There are lots of different buildings at Headcorn Aerodrome.

This is a maintenance hangar where the aircraft are kept and repaired.

The fire and rescue vehicles are also in the hangar, ready for emergencies.

A mechanic is working on this aeroplane engine

Engines can be so heavy that a crane is used to lift them.

Visitors, ground crew and pilots can go to the café for a snack

Before taking off, pilots must go to the office to pay their fees.

This pilot is ready to depart so he is checking the propeller

The pilot needs the propellor to pull the aeroplane through the air.

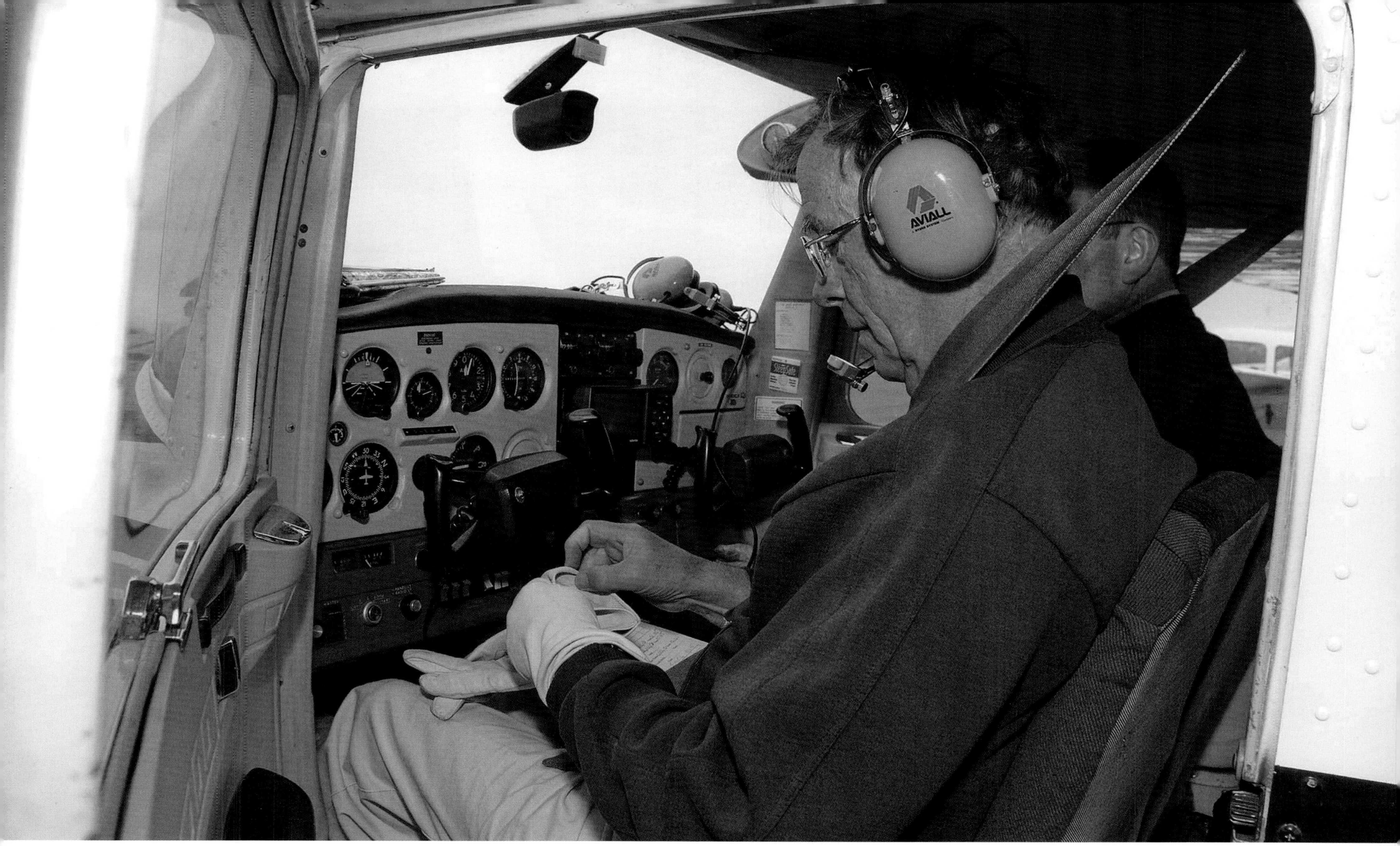

A pilot sits in the cockpit with his seatbelt and headset on

The cockpit has dials, instruments and a control column to steer the plane.

Using the control column the pilot can move the wing flaps up or down

The pilot uses the rudder to control the direction of the plane.

This is the undercarriage of the plane, where the wheels join the aircraft body

There are navigation lights on every plane, red on one wing, green on the other.

Special aviation fuel from the filling station is used to fill the plane's tank

The pilot speaks to air traffic control and waits at the holding point for take off.

This pilot is cleared for take off and accelerates down the grass runway

Back in the sky again! Goodbye. Fly safely.

What if...
We were pilots?

Ideas and Activities for Practitioners

Starter Activities

Starter activities could include:

- singing some of the songs or reading one of the themed stories;
- making one of the suggested visits;
- viewing the Powerpoint presentations from the CD-ROM (printed out, on your computer or on an interactive whiteboard);
- exploring the websites with the children;
- reviewing your existing resources and adding some from the resource list;
- brainstorming with the children to find out what they already know about pilots, planes and flying. Some may have a lot of experience as passengers;
- talking about local and national airports, using a map or globe if appropriate to the age of the children;
- when you are outside, looking for and listening to planes in the sky. Talk about where they might be going;
- telling a story such as 'Freddie Goes on an Aeroplane', 'Sadie the Airmail Pilot' or reading a non-fiction book such as 'Going on Holiday', 'A Day at an Airport' or 'A Day with a Pilot'.
- visiting a travel agent to collect some information about flights;
- talking about the many different ways we can fly – in a plane, a helicopter, a hot air balloon, a glider;
- printing some of the photos from the CD-ROM to make a simple display (or just put the CD in the computer for the children to look at);
- displaying some non-fiction books about pilots and their work.

Visits

It may be difficult to arrange a visit to an airport or aerodrome, so you may have to start this topic by asking someone to visit you.

Before you go on a visit or meet a visitor:

- Try contacting a local airport or airfield to see if someone can come to talk – small airfields are often able to be more flexible than the big ones.
- Look at some pictures, stories and books;
- Sing some of the songs;
- Prepare well for the visit by knowing what you want to ask;
- Prepare the children well. If you are having a visitor, look at some books and some of the photos on the CD, think of some of the things you want to find out and practise the questions;
- Find out if any of the children have experiences to share – have been on a plane, to an airport, met someone coming home?
- Do they know where the planes they see have come from and where they might be going?
- If you can't get a visitor to come, you may be able to take some photos when you are at an airport. Remember that you can only take photos in some areas of the building!

Watch some videos

- **http://www.flightlevel350.com** has a great video of flying upside down and looping the loop in a propeller driven plane and other video clips of planes taking off and landing
- **http://www.metacafe.com/watch/408878/airline_pilots/** - a video clip of a plane taking off from the cockpit
- **http://videos.howstuffworks.com** better video with pilot talking

These free video clips give a good idea of how planes work and will enable children who have not been on a plane to get some idea of the size and movements of planes.

During the preparation stage:

- You may want to work more closely with the children to discuss what happens at an airport, what all the people do, what makes planes fly, what is needed for a long flight on a plane and how all the things get on the plane. Make a pictorial or word list of everything you might need on a long journey.
- Talk about the different jobs involved in getting a plane ready – cleaners, baggage trolley drivers, bus drivers, people to load the food, someone to put out the magazines and the activity packs for children. Don't forget the food trolleys, the cutlery, the gifts and duty free trolley, even the loo paper and rubbish bags!
- Try making up a play about getting a plane ready. Make a plane from chairs, then everyone chooses a role, and works together to get the plane ready for the flight before the captain, crew and passengers get on board.

And some follow up:

- Talk about what you have seen, looking at any photos you have taken and anything a visitor has shown you, or what the children remember from stories and video;
- Use the children's suggestions about making a role play setting - what you need, where to make it, how to organise it;
- Collect some hats, jackets (old shirts dyed dark blue are really good for uniforms);
- The pilot and crew need food and drink - talk about how this happens, and who gets it ready for them.
- Set up a role play plane interior with trolleys and chairs with seat belts – the children will make suggestions of what they need;
- Make an airport terminal with a café, security screening, passports and tickets;
- Practise what the people say behind the airport counter, in security, and on the plane.

And if the pilot came to visit you:

- Talk about what they said and did, and look at photos and pictures in books or from the CD-ROM;
- Look at some websites for some ideas;
- Sing some more songs and rhymes together as you practise what pilots and their crew do.

Vocabulary

- airplane
- pilot
- co-pilot
- flight attendant
- jacket
- cap
- badge
- stripes
- uniform
- scarf
- count
- passenger
- cockpit
- cabin
- lights
- seat belt
- tray table
- arm rest
- light
- window
- curtain
- oxygen mask
- trolley
- case
- luggage
- X-ray machine
- tray
- food
- magazine
- safety card
- passport
- ticket
- boarding card
- duty free
- drink
- food
- video
- clouds
- take-off
- landing
- door
- aisle
- locker
- wings
- tailplane
- engine
- wheels
- toilet
- call bell
- announcement
- time
- gate
- bus
- steps
- runway
- helipad

HEALTH AND SAFETY!

Health and safety at any airport is really important, and children should understand why. It is always the responsiblity of the parent or carer to make sure a child is not left alone at any time in an airport as it is a potentially highly dangerous place. This includes gaming areas, restaurants and shops. A child should always be accompanied to the toilets and NEVER TALK TO STRANGERS!

MOST IMPORTANT RULE FOR CHILDREN:
If you get lost or separated from your group or family,
<u>GO STRAIGHT TO THE SECURITY OR INFORMATION DESK</u>
so they can make an announcement and find them for you.

SAFETY RULES TO LEARN FOR THE AIRPORT TERMINAL:

1. Pay attention to warning and information signs.
2. Listen to loud speaker announcements.
3. Try to find a map of the airport and make sure you know where the fire and emergency exits are.
4. Look out for airport security staff or police - they are always ready to help.
5. NEVER WALK AWAY FROM YOUR BAGGAGE! Never let anyone interfere with your bags.
6. Make sure all your baggage has your name and details on it.
7. Do not play on the moving equipment such as escalators, lifts or luggage belts.
8. Look out for 'wet floor' signs during cleaning.
9. Look out for vehicles and wheeled objects in the terminal such as baggage carts, trolleys, wheelchairs, cleaning wagons, security vehicles etc. They may not see you!
10. Stay with your parents or family at all times. Make sure you can see them and they can see you.

SAFETY ON A FLIGHT:

1. Pay attention as you enter the aircraft, know where your exits are. Count the rows of seats to the nearest exits, starting when you board the plane, then the over wing exits, and other exits throughout the plane. Your closest exit could be right behind you.

2. Read the in-flight safety card and make sure you know all the basics;
   - how to put your seatbelt on
   - where to store your hand luggage
   - how to put the life jacket on
   - the position to sit in your seat for an emergency landing

3. Listen to the flight attendant and pay attention as you follow the safety briefing. You will be shown how to do all the points in the safety card. Make sure you understand the lights and signs above your seat. Remember the information contained in the safety cards can save your life.

4. During take off and landing keep your seat belt fastened and your seat upright. Make sure your food tray is packed away. Do not move around the plane unless you need to.

5. What you wear is important. Wear comfortable, loose clothes with long sleeves - it may get cold on the flight.

6. Do not use remote control toys, your mobile phone or a computer. These can interfere with the aeroplane's equipment.

Arrivals

Role Play

Children will love being plane crew members, and this play particularly attracts those children who have already been on a plane. Try to get some real caps, and make some credible uniforms from shirts, with ties and scarves to make them look more realistic. Gold braid round sleeves and some badges made from gold card will enhance simple costumes and uniforms. Remember that the flight crew have special bags for their belongings and instructions.

Your role play setting might be:

- a reconstruction of the interior of a plane;
- a travel agent, check-in desk or ticket office
- a story place – from one of the plane, ballooning or helicopter stories you have shared.

Depending on where you start, the children will have plenty of ideas of the things they need, the place they want to play and how to organise the resources. Remember that domestic play will be a strong feature of any role play activity, so some children may be fascinated with serving meals, others with moving the bags around, or taking tickets. You could even incorporate your snack arrangements in the play setting.

Use photos you have taken or those on the CD-ROM to help with the decisions about what is needed and how it could be found, made, replicated or pretended. Children are very inventive, don't restrict their creativity by trying to make things look too much like the 'real thing'. Children will often use the most surprising substitutes for real life uniforms, equipment or food.

You could make a ticket office, use your outdoor area for baggage handling, make planes from equipment indoors or outside. Always offer mark making equipment – for checking passengers, looking up flight information, making notices, boarding cards, tickets and signs. Magazines and comics will be useful for in-flight reading.

Always ask the children what they think they would like and respond to their questions, requests and ideas about the play - this way, you may get some surprises, but you will certainly get a place that the children will get involved in and understand.

You could link this role play with projects or topics on Transport, Our Community, Holidays or A Sense of Place. It could also support Science, Technology, Geography and Citizenship in Key Stage 1.

Setting up the role play

Your role play setting can be indoors or out - or even in two places:

- a travel agent indoors and an airport outside;
- a house indoors with suitcases and bags to prepare for holidays;
- an airport complex complete with baggage, security, boarding and flights;
- a pilot's house indoors (for clothes, boots, sandwich box etc) and an airplane cockpit outside or in another place in your room.

Resource Suggestions

It need not be expensive to find creative items for role play - let imagination do the work! Don't forget to ask the children what they need for their play and don't provide everything at once - start small and add things as the children need them.

Free or sometimes donated if you or the children ask:

- card for labels, badges, signs and menus
- scrap paper for plans, tickets, boarding cards and notes
- small trolleys, bags and cases
- boxes from washing machines and fridges (to make control panels and ticket desk tops)
- old shirts to turn into uniform jackets
- magazines, brochures and papers with pictures of planes and travel destinations

Cheap, charity or bargain shop:

- plastic and paper plates, small trays and cups to use for in-flight meals
- note books, clip boards, post-its and pens
- chairs or plastic boxes for seats
- plastic sheets
- second hand cases and bags
- phones - mobiles, hands free and fixed
- maps and globes

Some things to include in your indoor/outdoor apparatus:

- screens and big boxes to make plane interiors
- some lightweight tables and chairs – look for children's outdoor furniture in sales, motorway service shops and garages
- rope
- trolleys and barrows for baggage
- signs and adverts for safety, directions etc

For the dress-up box:

- shirts for uniforms – cut off the collar and shorten the sleeves – then children can wear them back to front
- child-sized caps and hats
- reflective waistcoats for the ground crew

To make or find:

- small world vehicles to play out the role play small size in builders' trays
- booking diaries, messages, notices, signs
- maps, atlases and globes
- signs of all sorts
- catalogues and pictures of planes, uniforms, travel equipment, holiday brochures
- holiday clothes, suntan cream etc for packing in cases
- cable reels to make conveyers for luggage and security screening

Extending the Play

- Talk about the things pilots do, how they keep their passengers safe, how they work with their crew.
- Talk about what the co-pilot, the stewardess, the security officer, the passport inspector does.
- Talk about how pilots and crew clear up at the end of a flight, who cleans the plane and gets it ready for the next flight.
- Talk about different sorts of buildings and places at an airport – roads, car parks, shops, waiting areas, cafes, the control tower – look at the images on the CD-ROM and find things on the map.
- Contact your local newspaper (the press department), and see if they have any photos of unusual holiday stories, such as animals travelling. Find out how zoo animals travel, what about circus animals?
- Set up a plane at snack time and have your snack on flight trays – use the packaging from fruit and vegetables to make the plates.
- Talk about where the food on planes comes from – how is it kept fresh and healthy? How do they know how many meals to load? What about the captain and crew – where and what do they eat?
- Make a scrapbook of pictures of planes and of travelling – visit some travel agents for brochures.
- Join in the role play - be a nervous passenger, a new pilot or a fussy grandma!
- Set up some scenarios – bad weather such as fog or snow, the pilot not arriving, no food. Use these to talk about and work through problem solving situations.
- Do some sequencing, either with cards or photos (look on the CD-ROM for some photo sequences) and either talk them through or play sequencing games. Base these on building sequences: What happens first? What is under the ground? How does the water get to the tap? How do you make cement and then build a strong wall?
- Watch a video or DVD sequence of flying, and use it to help with introducing different scenes and situations.
- Get the children to advertise for a new pilot, luggage loader, flight attendant etc. Write an advert, interview applicants and train the new person.

Songs and Rhymes

- **I'M A LITTLE AIRPLANE - sung to 'I'm a Little Teapot'**

  Thank you Pam S. for this cute action song!

I'm a little airplane,
(children raise arms at sides to shoulder height.)
Now watch me fly!
(They spin one of their arms in front of them as if it were a propeller)
Here are my instruments
From down low to up high.
(With their other arm, they reach from the ground to above their heads.)
First I get revved up.
(Children make engine noises while still spinning their arms.)
Then I can fly,
(Children raise arms to shoulder height.)
Lifting off the runway
(They start walking forward.)
Up into the sky!
(They go up on their tiptoes and continue to move forward. Let them circle a while before returning to their airplane.)

I press on the starter,
The propeller whirls around
My airplane and I
Brush over the ground.
I lift from the field,
The motor roars out loud,
Far below is the earth,
Above me a bright cloud.
I dip and I drop
I swoop and I rise –
Oh, it's fun to be flying way up in the skies! (original positions)

• THE AIRPLANE

The airplane has great big wings:

(arms outstretched)

Its propeller spins around and sings, "Vvvvvv!"

(make one arm go round)

The airplane goes up:

(lift arms)

The airplane goes down:

(lower arms)

The airplane flies high

(arms outstretched, turn body around)

Over the town!

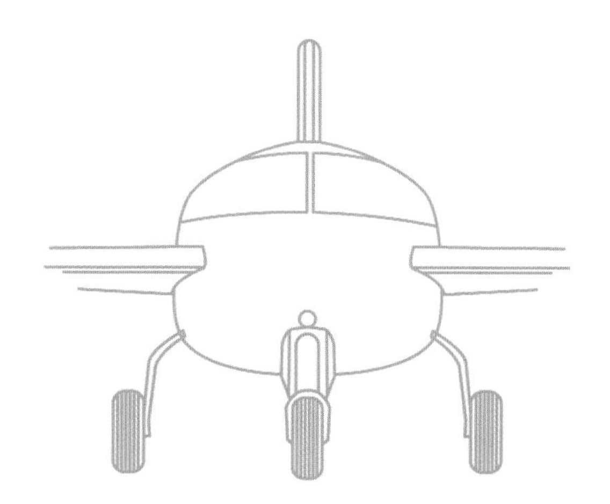

• THE AIRPLANE - sung to 'Did You Ever See a Lassie'

Did you ever see an airplane, an airplane, an airplane

Did you ever see an airplane way up in the sky?

There are big ones and small ones

And short ones and tall ones

Did you ever see an airplane way up in the sky?

• DOWN AT THE AIRPORT EARLY IN THE MORNING

See the little aeroplanes all in a row -

Watch when the pilot pulls on the joystick -

Swoosh, swoosh, zoom, zoom -

Off you go!

See the little helicopter waiting to go -

Watch when the pilot pulls on the joystick -

Whish, Whish, up, up -

Off you go!

• THE PROPELLERS ON THE PLANE - sung to 'The Wheels on the Bus'

The propellers on the plane go round and round
Round and round, round and round
The propellers on the plane go round and round
All through the sky

The pilot on the plane says Move On Back! Move On Back! Move On Back!
The pilot on the plane says Move On Back!
All through the sky

The people on the plane go up and down, up and down, up and down
The people on the plane go up and down
All through the sky

Substitute these lines:

* *The wipers on the plane go swish, swish, swish*
* *The seats on the plane go back and forth*
* *The lady on the plane says, "Get off my feet...."*
* *The baby on the plane goes, "Wa-Wa-Wa...."*
* *Use a child's name as in "Mark on the plane says, "Let me off!"*
* *The people on the plane said, "We had a nice ride...."*

• THE AIRMAN - original author unknown

rrrrrrrrrrrrr
The engine roars,
The propellers spins,
'Close the doors!'
Our flight begins.
zzzzzzzzzzzzzzzz
The plane rises;
it skims the trees.
Over the houses
We fly at our ease.
mmmmmmmmmmm
ZOOM goes the plane,
The engine hums.
Then home again,
And down it comes.

• ROCKETS AND AIRPLANES - sung to 'Twinkle Twinkle Little Star'

Rockets and airplanes flying high, (spread out arms, twist at waist.)
Flying fast up in the sky.
The Concorde makes a sonic BOOM! (clap)
A spaceship flies up to the moon.
Maybe someday I'll ride a jet,
Or be a pilot, better yet. (pretend to fly jet.)

• WE'LL BE FLYING HELICOPTERS! - sung to 'She'll be coming round the mountain'

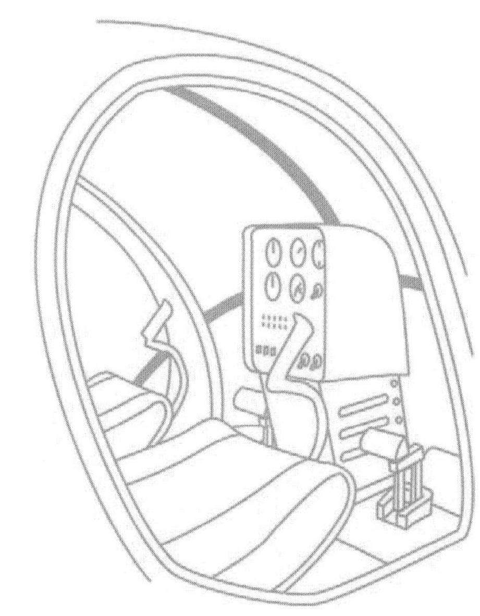

We'll be flying helicopters by ourselves!
We'll be flying helicopters by ourselves!
We'll have headsets, we'll have clipboards
We'll have coats with shiny buttons
We'll be flying helicopters by ourselves!

We'll be contacting the tower when we land
We'll be contacting the tower when we land
On our headsets we'll ask clearly
'Air traffic control can you hear me?'
We'll be contacting the tower when we land

We'll be filling up with fuel before we go
We'll be filling up with fuel before we go
At the office we'll pay money
at the café fill our tummy
We'll be filling up with fuel before we go

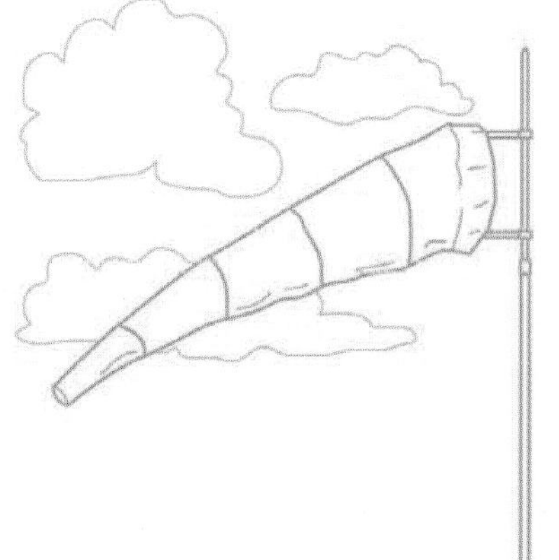

We'll be looking at the windsock in the sky
We'll be looking at the windsock in the sky
If its windy it is blowing
That's the only way of knowing
We'll be looking at the windsock in the sky

We are ready to take-off so here we go!
We are ready to take-off so here we go!
With a wave we say goodbye
Roaring engine up so high
We are ready to take-off so here we go!

Books and Stories

Title (Fiction)	Author	Publisher
Tough Stuff; Helicopter Rescue	Kate Hayler	Egmont
Sadie the Airmail Pilot	Kellie Strom	Picture Corgi
'Star Wars' Star Pilot	Laura Buller	Dorling Kindersley
Budgie, the Little Helicopter	Duchess of York	Simon and Schuster
Thomas and the Helicopter Rescue	Christopher Awdry	Egmont
The Fantastic Flying Journey	Gerald Durrell	Conran Octopus
Lettice the Flying Rabbit	Stanley	Picture Lions
Winnie's Flying Carpet	Valerie Thomas	OUP
Cinderella and the Hot Air Balloon	Ann Jungman	Frances Lincoln
Curious George and the Hot Air Balloon	H. A. Rey	Houghton Mifflin
The Red Balloon	Albert Lamorisse	Doubleday
The Hedgehog's Balloon	Nick Butterworth	Picture Lions
Kipper's Balloon	Mick Inkpen	Hodder
Room on the Broom	Julia Donaldson	Macmillan
Topsy and Tim Go on an Aeroplane	Jean Adamson	Ladybird
Freddie Goes on an Aeroplane	Nicola Smee	Orchard

Title (Non-Fiction)	Author	Publisher
Bush Pilot!: Flying High Over Australia	Robin Brode	Barron's
Violet the Pilot	Steve Breen	Dial Books
I Want to Be a Pilot	Dan Liebman	Firefly Books
A Day with a Pilot	Bob Woods	Child's World
Helicopter	Stuart Trotter	Rockpool
Planes and Helicopters	Clive Gifford	Usborne
Richard Scarry's a Day at the Airport	Richard Scarry	Random House
The Story of a Helicopter	Angela Royston	Kingfisher
Rescue Helicopters	Cynthia Roberts	Child's World
Pilot Your Own Rescue Helicopter	Paul Dronsfield	Tide Mill Press
Helicopters	Jeffrey Zuehlke	Lerner
Planes, Gliders, Helicopters	Terry Jennings	Kingfisher
Going on Holiday (My Family & Me)	Mary Auld	Franklin Watts
Going on a Holiday	Maureen Lewis	Collins
Busy Books: Busy Airport	Rebecca Finn	Campbell Books
Airport	Felicity Brooks	Usborne
A Day at an Airport	Sarah Harrison	Millbrook Press
Signs at the Airport	Mary Hill	Children's Press
At the Airport	Paul Humphrey	Franklin Watts
The Airport	Patricia J. Murphy	Pebble Plus
A Busy Day at the Airport	Philippe Dupasquier	Walker Books
A Day in the Life of a Flight Attendant	Harriet Hains	Franklin Watts
Let's Go by Hot Air Balloon	Anders Hanson	Sandcastle
Amazing Aeroplanes	Tony Mitton	Kingfisher

Websites and DVDs

PLEASE NOTE: The content of these sites has been checked, but the possible links from them are endless. Young children should always be supervised when using the internet to avoid any accidental clicking to undesirable sites.

Website addresses

Careers

http://www.ca.courses-careers.com/airlines.htm

http://www.andysairplanes.com/ - kids site with songs and video clips

http://www.pilotweb.aero a site for pilots with lots of information and even some real planes for sale!

GOOGLE planes

http://pbskids.org/barney/children/music/airplane.html - listen to a song by Barney

http://www.metacafe.com/watch/408878/airline_pilots/ - a good video clip of a plane taking off from the cockpit

http://videos.howstuffworks.com video with pilot talking

http://www.flightlevel350.com has great video of upside down and loop the loop in a prop plane and other video clips of planes taking off and landing

http://www.direct.gov.uk/en/TravelAndTransport/PublicTransport/AirTravel/DG_078169

DVDs

Some of these need a muti-region player, because they come from the USA. These are marked region 1. Most of the children's DVDs on planes and flying are produced in America.

Fact and Information

Fighter Pilot & ME [DVD] [2000] [Region 1~ John Raphael

The Big Adventure Series: The Big Plane Trip [DVD] [1994] [Region 1] ~ William van der Kloot

Big Machines 2 - Trucks And Planes [DVD] ~ Big Machines

The Big Plane Trip [DVD] [Region 1]

All About Airplanes/All About Helicopters [DVD] [2007] [Region 1]

Look At That Plane [1995] VHS ~ Jeff Rawle

Flight Deck, JumpSeat Productions part of MCM Publications Group, 9 Albert Park, Sandycove, Co. Dublin, Ireland. Tel: +353 1 2806407

Learn To Fly - The Private Pilot's Licence Explained [VHS]

Junior Pilot [DVD] [2004] [Region 1]

Fiction

Series of stories for younger children

Jay Jay the Jet Plane: Jay Jay's Sensational Mystery [DVD] [2006] [Region 1]

Jay Jay the Jet Plane: Jay Jay's Big Mystery [DVD] [Region 1] ~ Donna Cherry

Lots of stories about Budgie the helicopter, such as Budgie The Little Helicopter - The Air Show [DVD]

Those Magnificent Men In Their Flying Machines [1965] [DVD]

The Mr Men Show - Mr. Bump Presents: Trains, Planes and Dillymobiles! [DVD] [2008]

Brum - Airport And Other Stories [DVD] [1989] ~ Guy G.D.W. Harvey

The Koala Brothers - Ned The Pilot DVD ~ Jonathan Coleman

What if...
We were pilots?

What's on the CD-ROM?

The Photographs

On the CD-ROM there are two photo slideshow presentations of still photos with short text. One relates to the photo sequence in this book, the other is longer and more in-depth. The CD-ROM also includes a large bank of photos as single images. There are many ways to use these photos to enhance or extend your role play. Here are some ideas:

- Display the photo slideshow on a computer or on an interactive whiteboard. Use as a straight presentation, or children can revisit the whole sequence or parts of it independently as they play.
- Have a computer screen in or near the role play area with the slideshow running, or use as part of an interactive display of books and other equipment.
- Small groups could watch the slideshow with an adult, reading or following the text as they go.
- Older children could use the presentation as stimulus for writing their own stories about flying planes or a day at the airport.
- Print out a photo at any size, just open the one you want and send it to your printer.
- Import the photos into a Word document if you want to make books. Just open a Word document and import the image from the CD-ROM.
- Use the photos for games: crop sections of photos for a Spot the Detail game, make small versions for a sequencing game.
- Manipulate the images to make scenes with pilots or attendants in your setting, your children visiting the airport or stories of your own with characters you know.

The Artwork

The CD-ROM contains a series of specially drawn pictures, diagrams, posters and other artwork. These include:

- aircraft;
- a pilot with clothing and equipment;
- maps and diagrams;
- name tags, signs and symbols;
- writing frames and borders for stories and pictures.

Most of the artwork appears in black line and full colour, so you can print off the pictures you need. Some ideas for using the images:

- You could make matching games, lotto, Snap etc. by printing off the pictures and laminating them. You can make the pictures any size up to A4.
- Print the pictures so children can add extra figures, their own aircraft, speech bubbles or stories by drawing on the printed picture.
- You could also use a simple paint program on the computer to add to, adapt and manipulate the images.
- Print the dressing figures and let children stick the clothes on them – older children could name and write the different items of clothing and equipment.
- Use the images to make posters for display or to go in your role play area.
- Import the images into Word to make books and stories, using the pictures to illustrate them. Or you could print off black and white copies and photocopy them so children could colour them to make their own books.

The artwork can be used in many creative ways:

- Print them on A4 or A3 sheets for the children to talk about. Draw in extra aircraft, figures, speech bubbles etc.
- Project them on to a white sheet or a blank wall and paint round the shapes to make a background for role play or a display - depending on the size of the area available, you could create a mural or display board.
- Project them outside and draw round them with chalk (it's best to do this in a dark place or in the evening so you can see the projection). Then draw round the picture with playground chalk and let the children paint it in to make an outdoor role play area.

THE MURAL

- A facade which you can show on a computer or whiteboard, or project to create a mural in your setting.
- The Airport Departures background is an image that you can project at any size, up to the size of a whole wall. You could print this onto an OHP transparency and project it behind the role play area; you could show it on an interactive whiteboard and play in front of it; or you could project it onto a wall, sheet or shower curtain, draw round it and let the children help you paint your own background indoors or outside.

- Also available in black and white line for colouring in or to use as the template for a mural for painting.

AIRCRAFT

(Also available in black and white line)

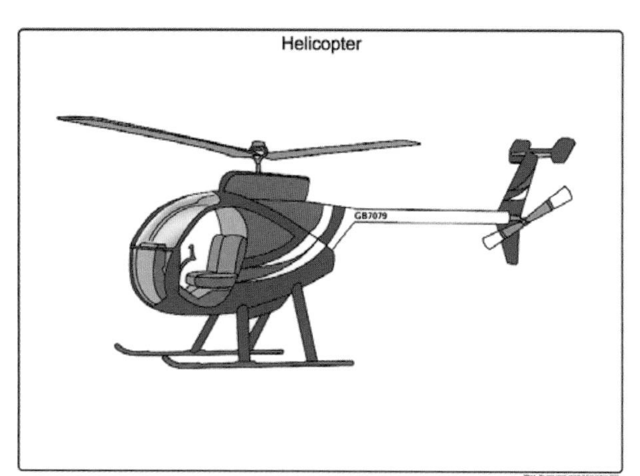

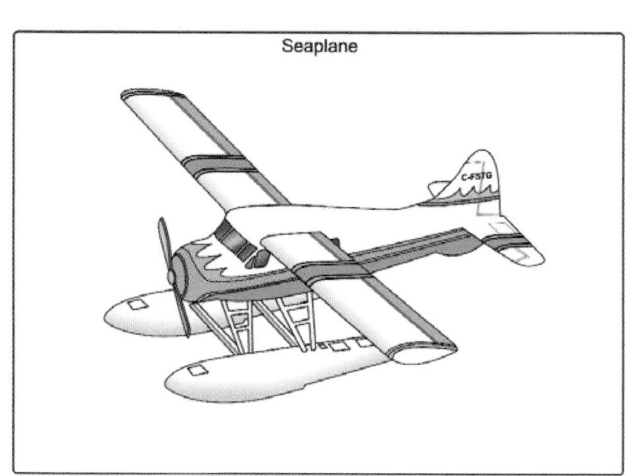

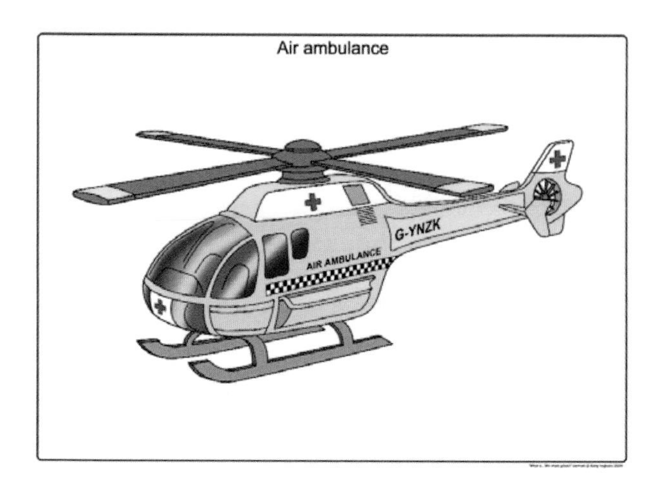

A PILOT'S CLOTHING

Line drawings of the items of clothing and equipment to use in different ways:

- Print the dressing figures and let the children stick the clothing on them.
- Older children could name and write the different items of clothing and equipment.

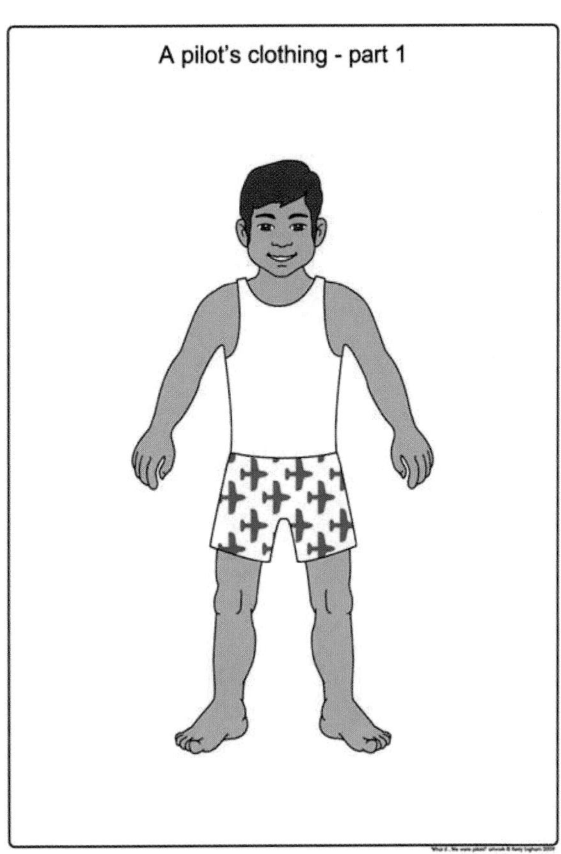

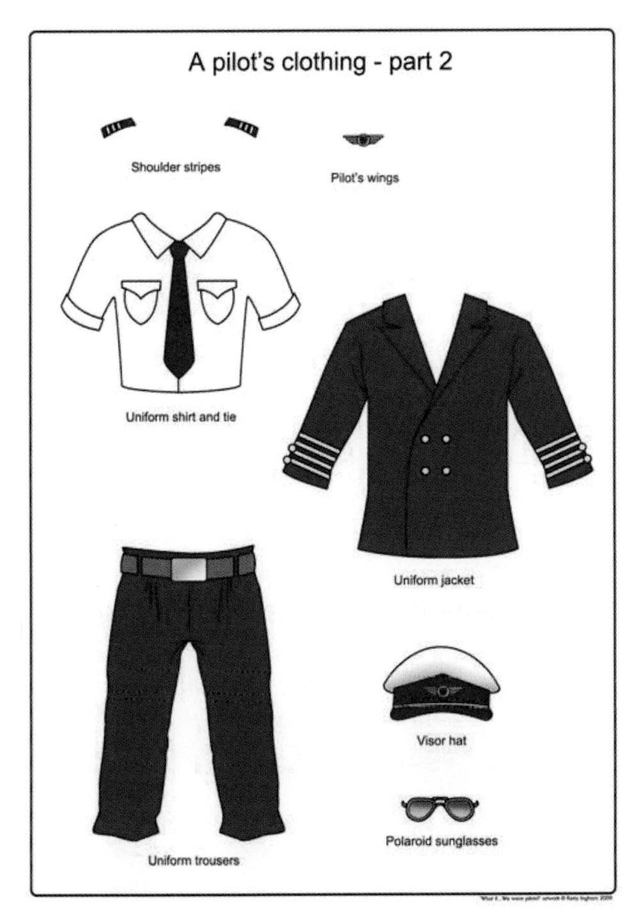

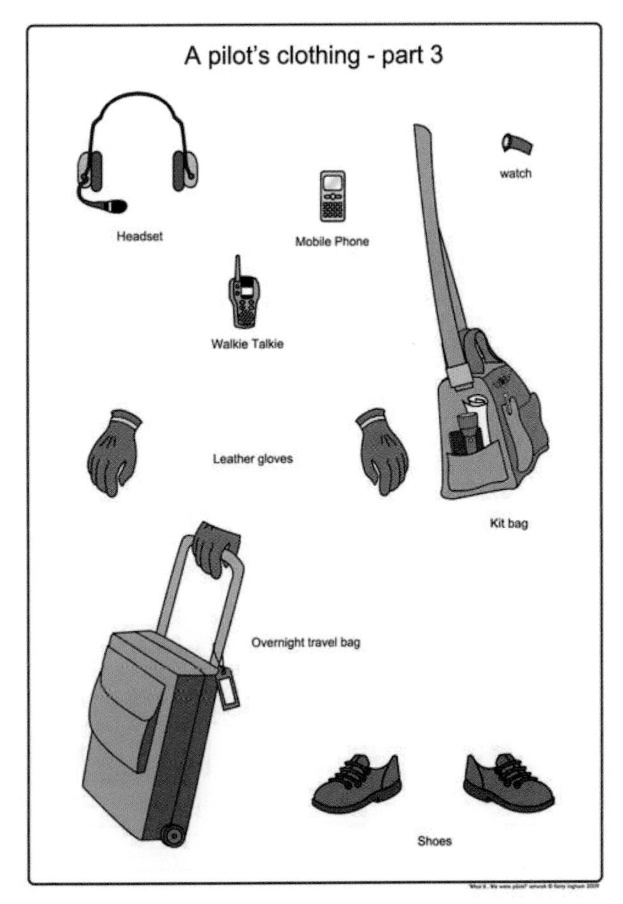

MAP OF AN AIRPORT

- The CD-ROM has a map showing the layout of an airport, including the runways, terminal building, aircraft maintenance hangers. car parks, flight training school and much more.

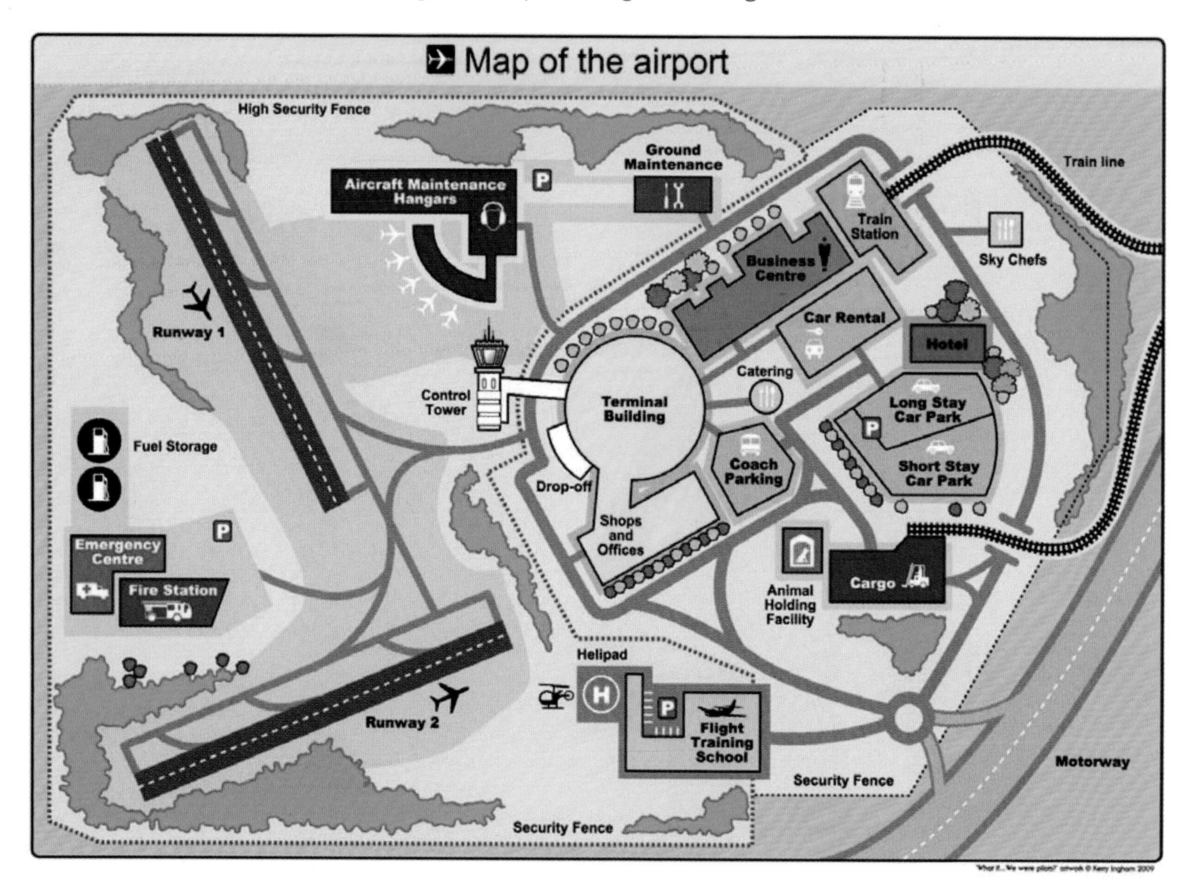

- Make a map of your own airport with the template supplied.

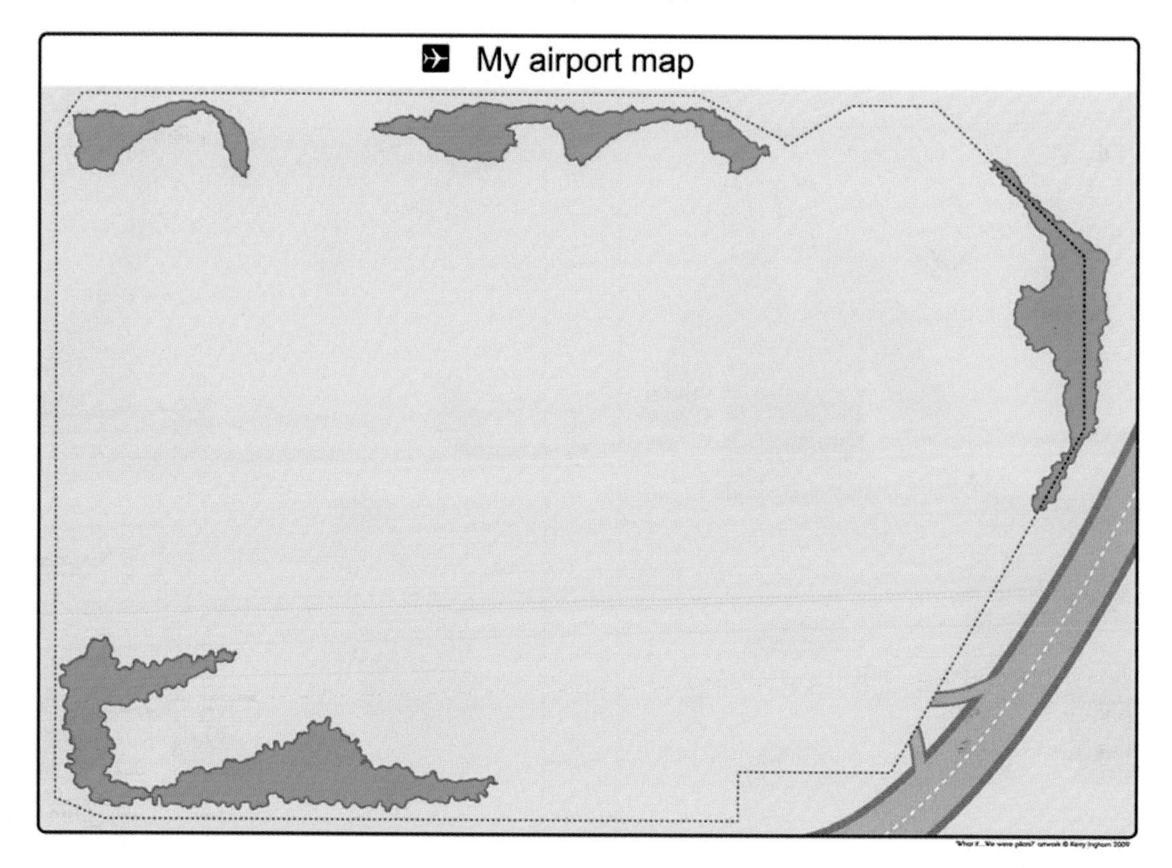

A-Z POSTER AND AIRPORT SIGNS

- A poster of airport and aircraft objects and equipment, including a full set in black and white line for colouring in and full colour sheets of airport safety signs and symbols.

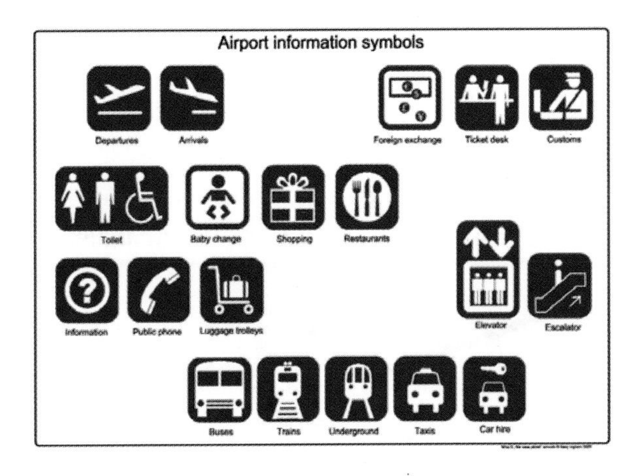

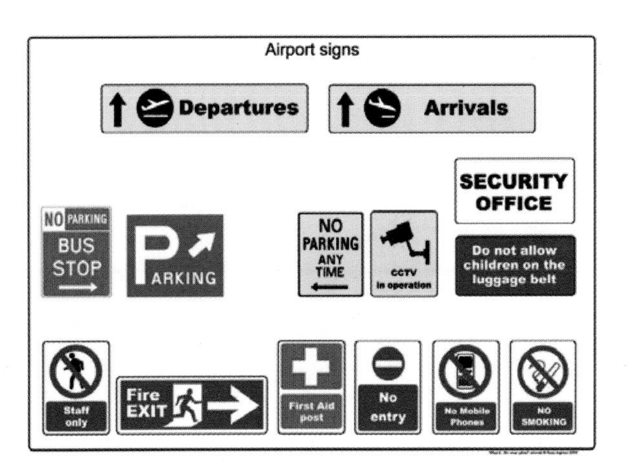

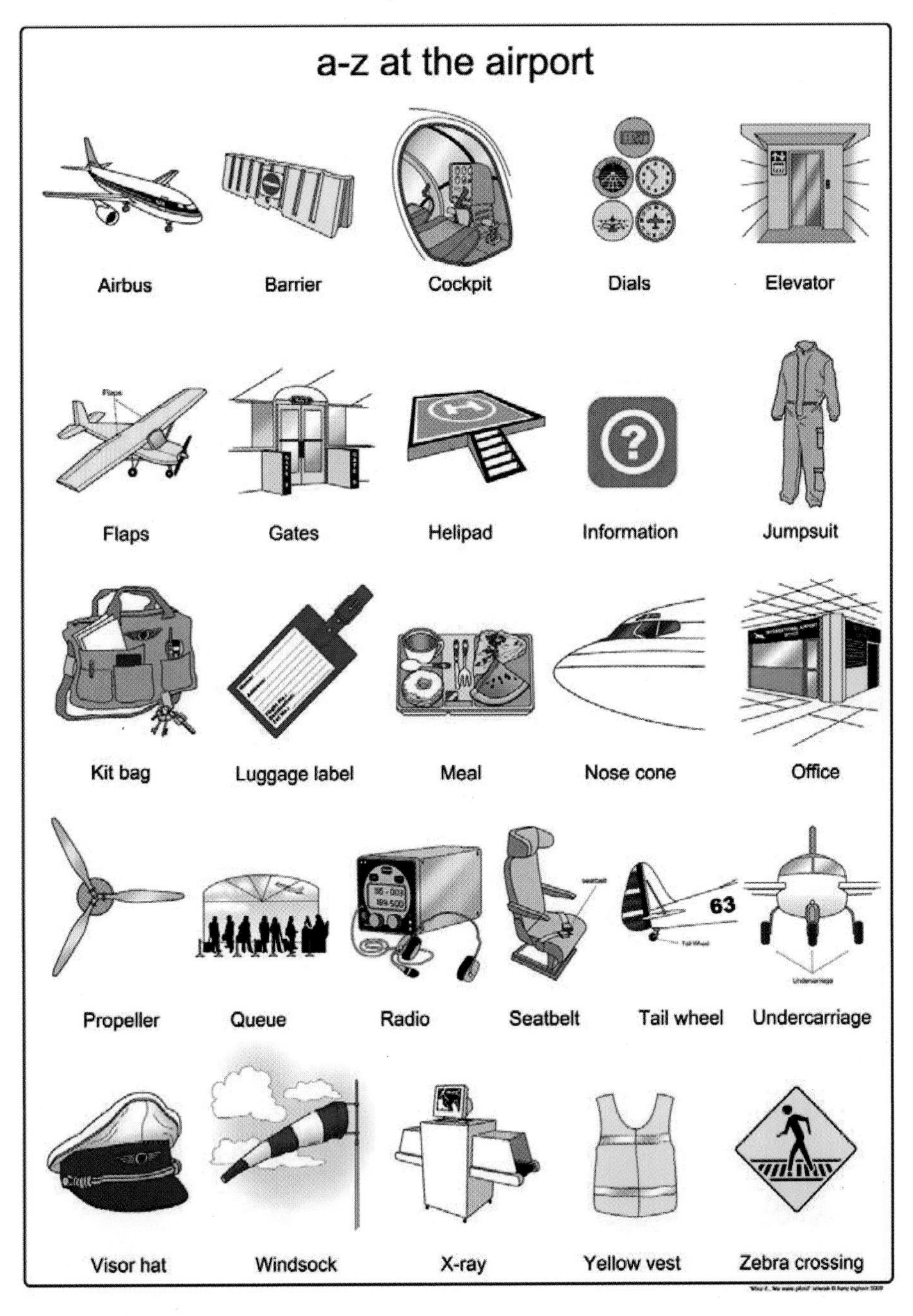

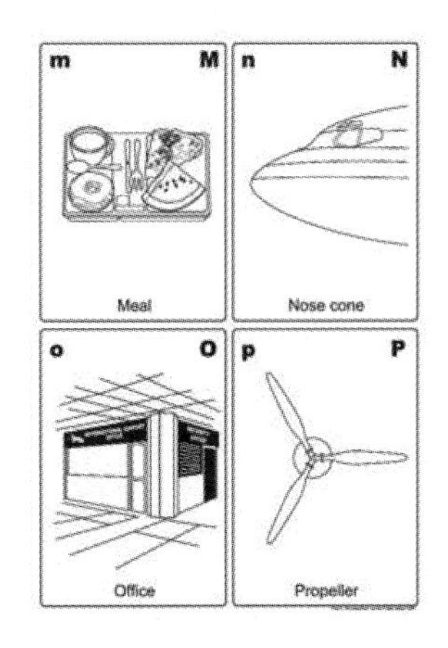

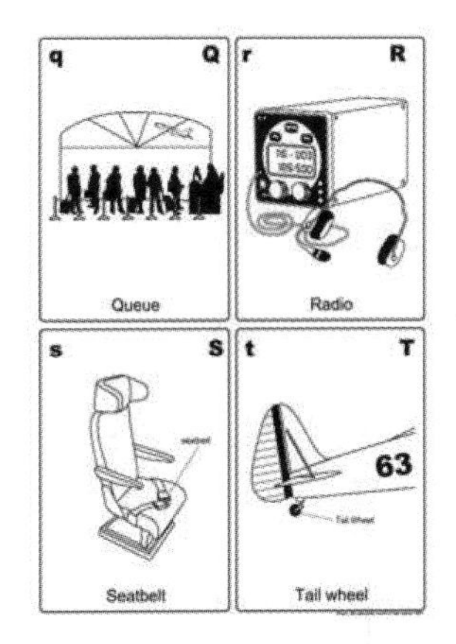

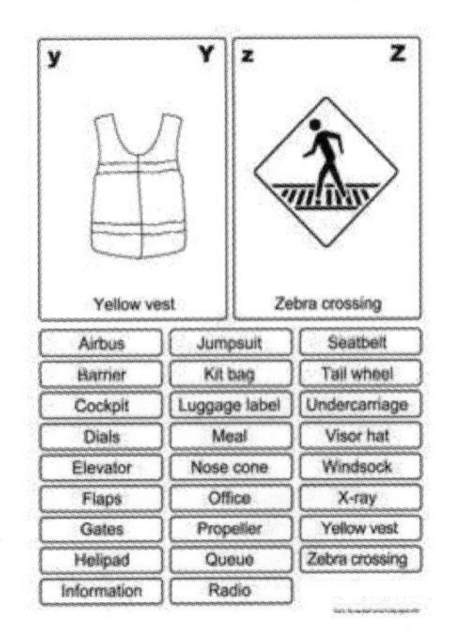

The Activity Sheets

The Activity sheets include:

- arrivals and departure charts with spaces for the children to fill in flight details;
- a colourful border design for pictures and writing;
- sequencing pictures with a series of spaces so children can record the steps to going on holiday and things to do at the airport;
- name tags with job titles at the airport;
- groundcrew vehicles to name;
- airport symbols to name.

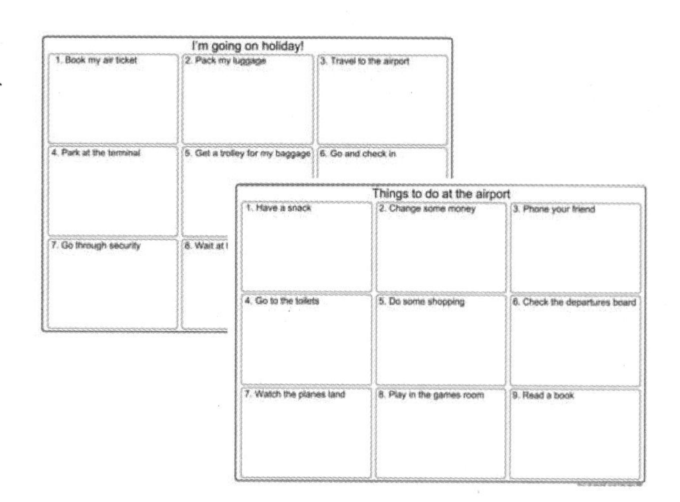

I'm going on holiday!

1. Book my air ticket	2. Pack my luggage	3. Travel to the airport
4. Park at the terminal	5. Get a trolley for my baggage	6. Go and check in
7. Go through security	8. Wait at t	

Things to do at the airport

1. Have a snack	2. Change some money	3. Phone your friend
4. Go to the toilets	5. Do some shopping	6. Check the departures board
7. Watch the planes land	8. Play in the games room	9. Read a book

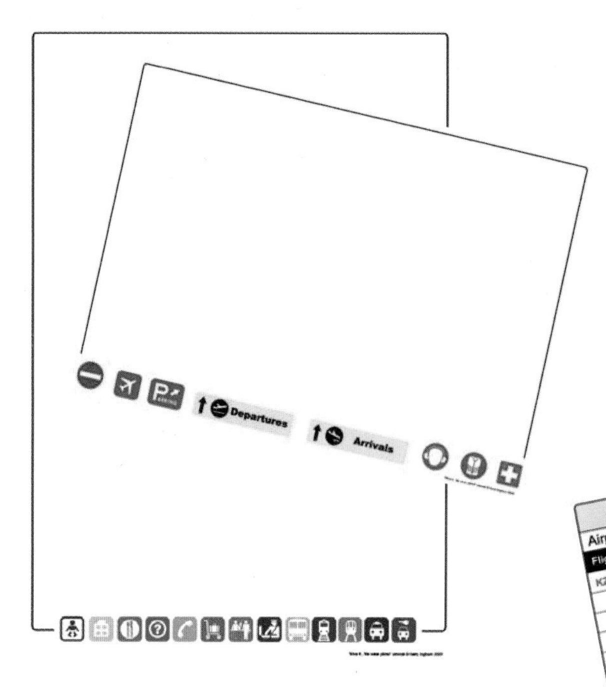

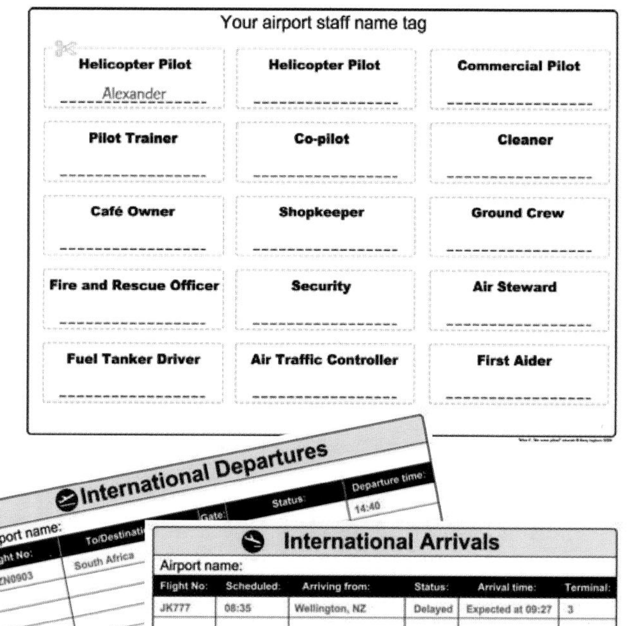

Your airport staff name tag

Helicopter Pilot	Helicopter Pilot	Commercial Pilot
Alexander		
Pilot Trainer	Co-pilot	Cleaner
Café Owner	Shopkeeper	Ground Crew
Fire and Rescue Officer	Security	Air Steward
Fuel Tanker Driver	Air Traffic Controller	First Aider

International Departures

Airport name:

Flight No:	To/Destinati	Gate:	Status:	Departure time:
KZN0903	South Africa			14:40

International Arrivals

Airport name:

Flight No:	Scheduled:	Arriving from:	Status:	Arrival time:	Terminal:
JK777	08:35	Wellington, NZ	Delayed	Expected at 09:27	3

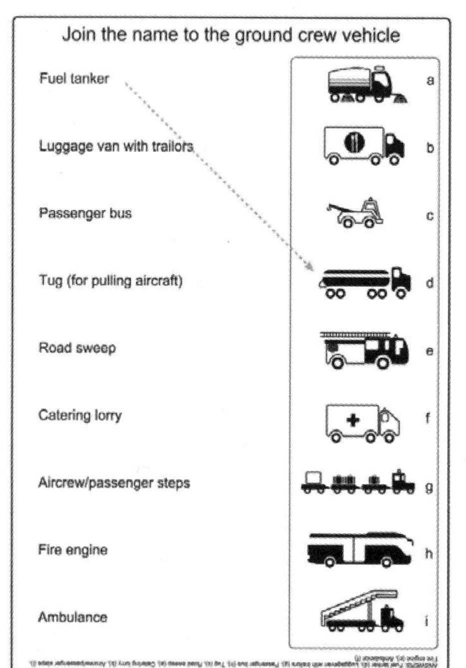

Join the name to the ground crew vehicle

Name	Letter
Fuel tanker	a
Luggage van with trailors	b
Passenger bus	c
Tug (for pulling aircraft)	d
Road sweep	e
Catering lorry	f
Aircrew/passenger steps	g
Fire engine	h
Ambulance	i

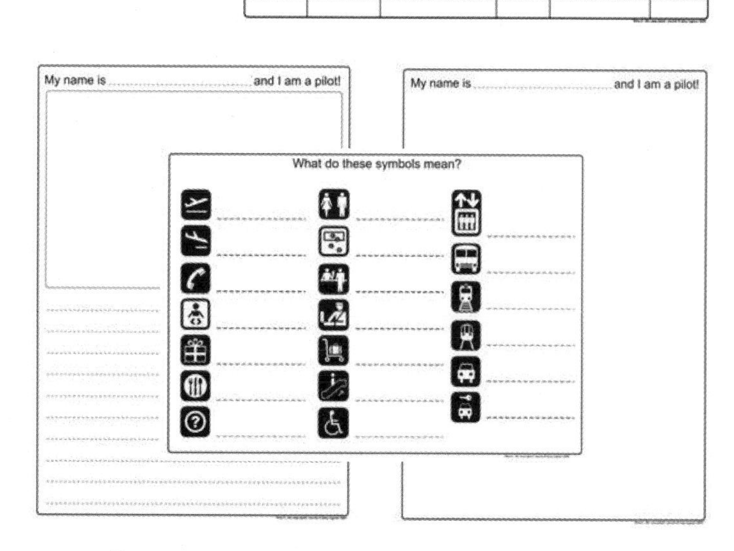

My name is .... and I am a pilot!

My name is .... and I am a pilot!

What do these symbols mean?